MARY ANN ALOYSIA
HARDEY
(1809 – 1886)

FIRST AMERICAN DAUGHTER

Ruth Cunningham, RSCJ
Revised edition by Carolyn Osiek, RSCJ

•

Mary Ann Aloysia Hardey (1809–1886)
First American Daughter

Copyright © 2025 Society of the Sacred Heart. All rights reserved. No part of this book may be used or reproduced by any means, graphic, electronic, or mechanical, including photocopying, recording, taping or by any information storage retrieval system without the written permission of the editor except in the case of brief quotations embodied in articles and reviews.

Cover illustration: Portrait photo c. 1873
Book design by Peggy Nehmen, n-kcreative.com

Printed in the United States of America
ISBN-978-1-7364924-7-5 (paperback) • 979-8-9946784-8-0 (ebook)

Published by:

4120 Forest Park Avenue
St. Louis Missouri 63108-2809
314-652-1500
www.rscj.org

 @RSCJUSC
facebook.com/SocietyoftheSacredHeart
facebook.com/ReligiousOfTheSacredHeart
(Vocations)

CONTENTS

Foreword by Ruth Cunningham v
Introduction to the Revised Edition vii
1. Beginnings: Maryland and Louisiana 1
2. Louisiana 7
3. New York and France 19
4. Responsibility 23
5. Foundations 31
6. Illness and Civil War 41
7. More Changes 47
8. Paris and America 51
9. Golden Conclusion 57
Appendix 65
Select Bibilography 69

CONTENTS

Foreword by Ruth Cunningham v
Introduction to the Revised Edition vii
1. Beginnings: Maryland and Louisiana 1
2. Louisiana 7
3. New York and France 19
4. Responsibility 23
5. Foundations 31
6. Illness and Civil War 41
7. More Changes 47
8. Paris and America 51
9. Golden Conclusion 57
Appendix 65
Select Bibiliography 69

FOREWORD BY RUTH CUNNINGHAM

This account of the life of Mother Mary Ann Aloysia Hardey, merely a sketch of her relationships and achievement, relies largely on letters now available in the general archives of the Society of the Sacred Heart in Rome and digitally in the provincial archives in St. Louis. The correspondence with Mother Madeleine Sophie Barat, especially, reveals Mother Hardey as a brilliant, sensitive woman, learning to deal with herself and others under the guidance of a saint. It shows a woman of great personal magnetism and balanced judgment, highly endowed for both practical and spiritual affairs, clear in her vision and magnanimous in her response. Pioneer, administrator, and educator, she founded twenty-five schools of the Sacred Heart in the United States, Canada, and Cuba.

Her life spanned most of the nineteenth century in a United States whose struggle for independence was still evolving—until the nation, finally united, stood free of the institution of slavery and of foreign domination. Mary Ann Aloysia Hardey was close to both: a child in Baltimore during the War of 1812; a young girl on the family plantation in Louisiana where slavery was a part of life; a young nun at St. Michael, buying one enslaved person for the convent, and enfranchising another; a Southerner living in the North during the United States Civil War. Mother Hardey traveled in every kind of wagon, boat and train, visiting her convents and schools from New York to Cincinnati, from Halifax to Havana. So much needed to be accomplished, and so soon, in the rapidly expanding countries. It was no wonder that she often traveled at night to save time. During her long, full life, she saw the train replace the covered wagon, the steamship replace the sailing vessel. If travel was slow, communication was slower. She complained to Mother Barat that her letters were a century in coming, even though by this time a letter to Europe could be sent and answered in one or two months, not the six months of Mother Duchesne's day; she longed for a "transoceanic telegraph" between Paris and New York to keep her informed. Telephones were still novelties in the 1870s, and even photography was still in process of development. Jet transportation and instant communication were a century too late for her.

At thirty-one, Mother Hardey was made responsible for a time, for all the convents of the Sacred Heart in America. She trained, supported, counseled, and led others to reach for the ideals that she herself cherished. Through all and above all a woman of deep prayer, she was single-hearted in her dedication to witness to God's love. Mother Mary Ann Aloysia Hardey was a Religious of the Sacred Heart whom Saint Madeleine Sophie Barat could claim with just pride as her "first American daughter." [1]

---

[1] Mother Hardey was not the first American to enter the Society of the Sacred Heart, but she was the first American that Saint Madeleine Sophie Barat knew intimately, the first whom she counseled and formed for the work she was to accomplish in America. Mary Ann Layton was the first American Religious of the Sacred Heart who entered and remained, beginning at Florissant August 19, 1820. As a novice, she accompanied Mother Eugénie Audé to the foundation of Grand Coteau, Louisiana, in 1821, where she made her first vows on June 6, 1822. Mary Ann Hardey would have been present for the ceremony as a student in the school.

INTRODUCTION TO THE REVISED EDITION

As vice-vicar and then superior vicar[2] of the East, Mary Ann Aloysia Hardey, RSCJ, was responsible for foundations up and down the eastern coast of the United States, in Canada, and in Cuba. As first American assistant general, she brought the lived experience of the Americas to the motherhouse in Paris. Her correspondence with and spiritual guidance from Mother General Madeleine Sophie Barat began as early as 1836, and their relationship deepened after their first meeting in person in France in 1840. It continued until Madeleine Sophie's death in 1865.

In view of the creation of the new province of ANAM (Antilles-North America-Mexico), it has seemed good to publish a revision of the short biography of Mother Hardey, first composed by Ruth Cunningham, RSCJ, published privately in typescript by the Society of the Sacred Heart at Kenwood, Albany, New York, in 1981.

Ruth Marie Cunningham, born in New York in 1913, grew up with mother, aunts, and sisters educated at the Sacred Heart. She attended school at Maplehurst in New York, then spent some

---

2 From 1851 to 1970, the international Society of the Sacred Heart was administered in governmental units called vicariates, each governed by a superior vicar.

time at Manhattanville College before entering the Society of the Sacred Heart in 1934. Her sister Frances had preceded her into the Society. Ruth served in most of the houses of the then New York Province before becoming professor of English at Manhattanville. After 1975, she lived at Kenwood in Albany, New York, and engaged in research and writing on Society history. She died there in 2005.

Prior to that of Ruth Cunningham, there were three major biographies of Aloysia Hardey. The first was in French by Marie Augustine Dufour (1823-1904), secretary general for twenty-six years, first for Mother General Josephine Gœtz (1868-1874), then for her successor Mother Adèle Lehon (1874-1894). During these years, Mother Dufour had access to primary sources and composed several biographies of important RSCJ of her time. Msgr. Baunard, who wrote the first published biographies of Madeleine Sophie Barat and Philippine Duchesne, considered her his collaborator in research. After him, she continued the tradition by writing anonymous privately published French biographies of Mothers du Rousier, Charbonnel, Gœtz, Lehon, and *Vie de la Révérende Mère Mary Ann Aloysia Hardey, Assistante Générale de la Société du Sacré-Cœur de Jésus* (privately published by the motherhouse, no date).

The second biography of Mother Hardey was that of Mary Garvey, RSCJ (1845-1932), first published in 1910: *Mary Aloysia Hardey*. New York: America Press, 1910. Mary Garvey, born in Ireland, came to New York as a child. After final profession in 1868, she was mistress general (head of the school) and superior in various houses, then vicar of the central vicariate in 1889. She died at Eden Hall in 1932. There was a second edition by Longmans, Green and Company in 1925, to coincide with the canonization of St. Madeleine Sophie.

The third biography of Mother Hardey was that of Margaret Williams, RSCJ (1902-1996), *Second Sowing: The Life of Mary Aloysia Hardey*. Sheed & Ward, 1942. The name of Margaret Williams is well known to anyone in search of Society history. Born in Connecticut in 1902, she spent her childhood on the west coast of the United States but returned to the east to attend Manhattanville College. She entered the Society in 1924 and later taught for thirty-four years at Manhattanville College. She then embarked on several years living and teaching in the Far East Province of the Society before retiring to Kenwood in 1981. Her biographies and historical writings reveal her understanding of extensive literary and historical contexts as well as biographical details.

The present volume is a lightly revised edition of Ruth Cunningham's work, where necessary updated and clarified. It is planned to be available during the process leading to the new province of ANAM, given Mother Hardey's wide footprint in the foundations of the Society in its participant countries.

Use of the words America and American occurs in the original text of Cunningham, and in most of the literature on this context, in varied ways: sometimes in a general way as the land on the other side of the Atlantic from Europe, sometimes as North America, sometimes as the Society's foundations in Canada, United States, and Cuba. As far as possible, the original terms are maintained, to be interpreted from context.

1

BEGINNINGS: MARYLAND AND LOUISIANA

CHILD

Mary Ann Hardey was born on December 8, 1809, in the town of Piscataway, Maryland. She was the second of the eight children of Frederick Hardey and Sarah Spalding, both of old Maryland families. Mary Ann's paternal grandfather traced his ancestry to Nicholas Hardey, one of the founders of the original colony of Maryland by English Catholics in 1634. It was he who changed his name from Hardy to Hardey to distinguish his family line from another that was Protestant.

Travel and excitement characterized Mary Ann's life from the outset, for at the age of one, she was taken to the home of Grandmother Spalding in Baltimore to avoid a whooping-cough epidemic. Charming all by her precocious intelligence, she became the center of attention in the household. She remained four years in Baltimore, unable to see her mother during this time, for the Second War for Independence had begun. British soldiers now roamed the countryside, rendering travel even for short distances extremely dangerous. In the summer of 1814, as General William Winder collected his troops at Piscataway and nearby towns, excitement and anxiety were at a peak. On September 12, Baltimore felt the immediacy of danger when the flames of burning Washington, only forty miles away, warned of struggle yet to come. Baltimore waited, while Fort McHenry, its flag still flying, withstood the British bombardment for four days. The alert child of five must have shared the tension and fear of those around her, experiencing a sense of isolation and danger. Only when the invaders pulled out to sea did Mary Ann return home to Piscataway. Home seemed strange with two new sisters to claim part of her mother's attention, and Mary Ann became shy and reserved. This was only for a time, for often she recalled her mother's strong educative influence on her childhood.

Two years later, Mary Ann went on a much longer journey, and excitement was of a happier kind. The Hardey family was moving to a plantation in Louisiana where her uncle Charles had earlier emigrated. Baggage, furnishings, and animals were loaded on covered wagons, and the whole household—parents, children, and enslaved families—set off on a long trip of three to four months. In this fashion they crossed the Allegheny Mountains to Pittsburgh; then, by flatboat and steamer, they traveled down the Ohio and Mississippi Rivers to New Orleans.

Their plantation was in Opelousas, and once settled there, they must have been happy in their new surroundings, as we may judge from a letter that Sarah Hardey, Mary Ann's mother, wrote to her sister in Maryland, urging the whole family to follow her south.[3]

---

3 Letter begun December 12 and finished December 20, 1820. Sarah Hardey recommends after her father's death, that her sister Ellen "take care of the books our father procured for the instruction of his children." Garvey, 9-10.

EDUCATION

At home Mary Ann was taught by her mother, learning with her quick intelligence something of the practical art of managing a plantation. "Mis' Mary" soon became a favorite. At the age of eight she was allowed to make her First Communion, for when she attended classes with her sister, she was the one who could give all the answers. In 1821, her sister Ann went to school in Emmitsburg, Maryland, but Mary Ann was sent to the "Institute for the Education of Young Ladies," a new school opened that year by the Religious of the Sacred Heart at nearby Grand Coteau. Tuition posed a problem, for planters had more land than cash. Practical Mary Ann was ready with a solution: why not send some of the Hardey enslaved women to help with the school laundry? Her father took the suggestion, and Mary Ann Hardey became one of the first pupils of the Sacred Heart in Louisiana. The school, headed by Mother Eugénie Audé, numbered seventeen pupils in 1822. Mary Ann excelled in studies; she quickly learned French so that Mother Audé could speak to her in her native language instead of in hesitant English. Mary Ann, a natural leader, read the address of welcome to Mother Philippine Duchesne when she visited the school on August 6, 1822. Mary Ann liked to recall that her leadership was not always admirable, as when Bishop William Dubourg[4] made his first visit to Grand Coteau. While Mother Audé was greeting him at the door, the children led by Mary Ann Hardey ran from their ranks to hide under the stairs. But by the time

---

4   Louis William Valentin Dubourg (1766-1833), born in Saint-Domingue, was ordained in Paris in 1790. In 1815 he was named bishop of Louisiana, the entire area of the Louisiana Purchase of 1803. He returned to France in 1826.

she had finished school she was awarded the First Medallion for good conduct and leadership.

Mary Ann was graceful and energetic of movement, tall, blond, and gray-eyed. Her smile attracted others, and her frank, simple manner put them at ease. At home she must have been a gracious addition to the social life of brothers, sisters, and friends.[5] One evening before a party when she was fifteen and a half, she decided to enter the Society of the Sacred Heart. She excused herself from the event and set about making her plans. Her mother knew that with Mary Ann, a decision once made was final, but her father tried to change her mind. Still hoping to see her home in a week, he offered to drive her himself the few miles to the convent at Grand Coteau. He smiled as they said goodbye at the door of the convent, when Mary Ann asked him to send her the mirror she had forgotten.

NOVICE

Though the community at Grand Coteau had not been warned of her arrival, they welcomed their former pupil with joy, never doubting her vocation, for Mary Ann usually considered well before making a decision. But one instance when she acted on impulse occurred shortly after her entrance. Hoping to entice her home, "Old Aunt Sophie," one of the Hardey enslaved women, brought Mary Ann word that her father was ill. As the carriage rolled away from the convent, Mary Ann was in anguish. If her father needed her, she must go at once. With

---

[5] Many years later, Mother Hardey's younger brother Charles recalled: "She was my good angel, my playmate ...gentle, loving, full of attention." *Vie de la Révérende Mère Mary Aloysia Hardey.* n.d. (Private Printing.) pp.19-20 (Author's translation). Hereafter, this will be referred to as *Vie.*

no second thought and informing no one, she started walking home. Leaving the convent would mean that she would have to begin again as a postulant. As she walked, reason asserted itself, and after about a mile forced her to retrace her steps. It turned out that this had been only a ruse of "Aunt Sophie" to draw her home. When Mother Audé heard of it, she welcomed Mary Ann a second time.

Mother Audé's mission was to perpetuate the spirit of the Society of the Sacred Heart that she had brought to America in 1818. She did it well, and Mary Ann Hardey, though not yet sixteen, was exceptionally responsive.[6] The time as a postulant was shortened for Mary Ann to less than a month, and she received the habit on October 22, 1825. It was a custom promoted by Mother Philippine Duchesne for a new novice to take the name of a Jesuit saint,[7] so Mary Ann chose the name of "Aloysia."[8] This she used for the rest of her life.

---

6   Eugénie Audé entered the Society of the Sacred Heart in Grenoble, France, in 1815 and made her first vows in 1817. She made her final profession less than a year later, February 8, 1818, the morning of the day she left for America with Mother Philippine Duchesne. She held Mary Ann Hardey's gifts in high esteem, writing to Mother Barat: "One of the novices, Mary Ann Hardey, called 'Aloysia,' is very likely to succeed with the children; her appearance, her aptitude for studies, her docility when advice is given to her, her excellent judgment, her attachment to the Society" give great hope for the future. "I think that she will be a great help to us some day." *Vie*, p. 32.

7   Before Adeline "Gonzague" Boilvin became a novice in 1828, Mother Duchesne wrote to her: "Choose Louis, Louisia, Gonzague, for Aloysia has already been taken." Letter of December 31, 1828.

8   Through the name "Aloysia," author Ruth Cunningham discovered an interesting link in her own family with Aloysia Hardey. Her mother Blanche Donnelly, confirmed at Manhattanville in 1888, two years after Mother Hardey's death, chose "Aloysia" as her confirmation name. This was probably at the suggestion of one of the religious who had known and revered Mother Hardey.

Understanding Mary Ann's need to be active, Mother Audé provided time for horseback riding "for her health,"[9] but the day after becoming a novice, she was plunged into other activity. Mother Audé was leaving to make a foundation at St. Michael, Louisiana, about sixty miles from New Orleans, on the left bank of the Mississippi, and Mary Ann was to be one of the three religious and three novices to accompany her. They set out on October 23, 1825, and after a journey of forty-eight hours, they arrived to find their new house without a roof. Father Charles de la Croix vacated his parish house for them for several weeks. But when they moved into their convent, it still lacked chimney, stove, and even chairs. This first experience of foundation life prepared Mary Ann to cope with the inevitable privations entailed. There would be many such ventures in the years ahead.

Mary Ann had said that she was ready for anything required of her except teaching, but this was to be her work for the next seventeen years. She soon grew to love it. Novice though she was at the beginning, she appeared to the pupils as the ideal religious. Her manner gained respect; her way of treating all without distinction won their trust and love. Former pupils recalled later her vivid accounts of the early days of the Society, and her gift of inspiring others with love of the Sacred Heart.

---

9   Horseback riding, sea bathing, and travel were regularly prescribed for the health in the early nineteenth century.

2

LOUISIANA

ST MICHAEL

Mary Ann "Aloysia" Hardey had been a novice for only fifteen months, when on March 15, 1827, she was allowed to make her first vows. She was needed to replace the mistress general, Mother Xavier Hamilton,[10] who had become seriously ill. Meanwhile, Mother Duchesne, about to open a new school in St. Louis, wanted Aloysia there. Mother Audé quickly quenched that hope by writing to Mother Duchesne, "If you take Aloysia, you might as well take the whole community."[11] The history of the Society of the Sacred Heart in America would have been very different if she had gone to St. Louis at that time. If she had been in St. Louis, she would have turned to Mother Duchesne for advice

---

10 Mathilde (Xavier) Hamilton (1802-1827) and her sister Eulalie (Regis) came from Sainte Genevieve, Missouri, to the boarding school at Florissant in 1819. She made final vows in 1825 to be part of the foundation group at St. Michael, where she held positions of responsibility until her sudden death on April 1, 1827. Her sister Regis remained in St. Louis and held several important positions there, in northern cities, and in Canada, including that of superior at St. Charles at the time of Philippine Duchesne's death there.

11 *Vie*, 42.

St. Michael, first house, 1825. Parish church on right.

rather than to Mother Barat, her superior general in Paris. Instead, correspondence with Mother Barat was to become the great formative influence on her life. In managing the school and the house, Mother Barat told her, "In everything follow the government of your Mother Eugénie who has succeeded so well in that country."[12] She profited from Mother Audé's free and expansive direction, as Mother Duchesne later realized.[13]

In her new charge of mistress general, "Aloysia," now Mother Hardey, was showing strength, while winning the pupils by her sensitive kindness. In two years, the school at St. Michael numbered sixty-two pupils. This pleased Mother Duchesne when she made her first visit to St. Michael for a provincial council in 1829. Mother Hardey acted as secretary during those weeks and was in close touch with Mother Duchesne.[14] Though at times the

---

12 Letter of December 4, 1836, naming her superior at St. Michael.

13 June 9, 1844. Mother Duchesne tells Mother Boilvin that she is like Mother Hardey, "that beloved daughter of Mother Eugénie, called to carry on a work like hers; and how well she did it."

14 This was the last time that Mother Duchesne and Mother Hardey met, although as treasurer of St. Michael, Mother Hardey regularly sent money to her in St. Louis.

ST. MICHAEL'S CONVENT,

St. Michael, 1838

old French missionary reproved the young nun for her "American pride,"[15] she later wrote of her, "Aloysia is too perfect; she cannot live long."[16] Fortunately this prophecy proved incorrect.

A tragic cholera epidemic struck St. Michael in May 1833. Pupils were sent home; novices were evacuated to a remote wing of the convent. Mother Hardey moved among the sick and dying, assisting Mother Audé in giving comfort and in rendering service. She saved the life of one of the orphans by applying "common sense" remedies for twenty-four hours consecutively, after the doctor had pronounced the case hopeless. Her presence of mind and efficiency combined with gentleness to bring consolation to many. The bitter experience and complete self-giving of those days was deemed sufficient preparation for Mother Hardey to make her final profession on July 19. Mother Audé describes the profession ceremony to Mother Barat as "a flash of happiness

---

15 *Vie*, 45.

16 *Vie*, 40.

following the sad days I had just passed through."[17] The strain of this difficult time had been great for Mother Audé, but by vote of the religious in America, she was named assistant general in 1834, to visit all the houses and report to Paris. Once there, she did not return, for reasons of health.[18]

Her departure left St. Michael without a superior. Mother Audé had recommended Aloysia for the position, for she possessed "prudence, virtue, talents, all that it takes to be at the head, if you would pass over her age."[19] But Mother Barat judged twenty-three to be too young, and instead, she was given the charge of assistant to Mother Julie Bazire,[20] in addition to the offices she already held—those of mistress general, treasurer, and mistress of class.

PROBLEMS

Trouble with the trustees of the parish at St. Michael was about to erupt. A spirit of ill-will toward the convent may have stemmed from the fact that town and parish were never as prosperous as the school. Whatever the cause, the trustees objected when a wall was built on church-owned land between the convent and the adjacent church to form a kind of cloister for the religious. The trustees accused Mother Bazire and Mother Hardey of sacrilege, among other things. About fifty men were sent to break down the offensive wall, and the two religious

---

17 *Vie*, 48.

18 However, she then founded the house at Marseilles and went on to be superior at the Trinità dei Monti in Rome, where she died in 1842.

19 *Vie*, 48.

20 Julie Bazire (1806-1883) entered the Society in France and came to America in 1829. After being superior at LaFourche, then St. Michael, then Grand Coteau, she returned to France and left the Society.

were summoned to court. Before the case was heard, however, the trustees were persuaded to apologize, and to promise the convent tenure until a suitable location for the now flourishing school could be obtained.

Soon Mother Bazire needed to be replaced as superior. Aloysia had made her final profession July 19, 1833, so that she could fill that role. She wrote at that time to Mother Audé, "We shall learn to be more prudent and circumspect to keep any complaint at a distance."[21] She was prudent, but not prudent enough.

Inexperienced, she tended to be over trustful of others. That same year a desirable property was to be sold at auction. She acted swiftly to purchase the Landry estate for a new school. She planned a building of splendid proportions, large enough to accommodate 300 pupils. Hearing of this, Bishop Anthony Blanc of New Orleans voiced disapproval of its size, forbidding the completion of a building on that scale, for he feared unfavorable competition with the Ursuline school in his city. Mother Hardey had recourse to Mother Barat, whose ill-fated reply was copied by a trusted "friend of the convent," and shown to the bishop. In it, Mother Barat threatened to remove all her religious from his diocese if the bishop continued his objections, as their work in the Church would be curtailed.[22] Bishop Blanc confronted Mother Hardey with the letter, angrily denouncing her, Mother Barat and the whole Society of the Sacred Heart. For once, Mother Hardey's calm and self-possession left her, and she wept without restraint.[23]

---

21 In a letter to Mother Hardey in 1844, Mother Barat urges the greatest severity in the reception of novices and attention to their formation. She recalls Mother Hardey's imprudence at St. Michael when she "kept for so long a cruel wolf" in her sheepfold.

22 "We should be free to follow our vocation; bishops should support us in a good work, not limit it." Mother Barat to Mother Hardey, October 30, 1837.

23 *Vie*, 70.

Later the bishop was appeased and allowed the new school building to continue as planned. It was not yet completed when Mother Hardey was called to New York to start a foundation there. Her work at St. Michael had been crowned with success, although there had been much suffering entailed. Before she left, a lawsuit over title to the Landry estate was settled in favor of the Society.

The school was flourishing. Many of the novices trained there did honor to the spirit they received.[24] Mother Hardey had grown through her experiences. She had learned how to deal with people and to cope with difficult situations. Through it all she had counted on Mother Barat's guidance.

MOTHER BARAT

During her first years as superior, Mother Hardey felt very much alone, and looked to Mother Barat in Paris for advice and strength. A letter from her "gives me courage for a month," she wrote on July 12, 1837. The correspondence between them had begun somewhat formally in 1834 when Aloysia gave an account of her office as assistant, but by the time she accepted that of superior two years later, she was completely at ease. Overcoming her reluctance to take on the burden of government, she had written: "I will not resist any longer. As a true American I promise you, if to succeed I have only to follow your advice, I assure you in advance of success" (December 5, 1836).

She was completely open and frank in her letters, and Mother Barat's replies were equally so. "I love the simplicity and confidence

---

24 Among those trained by Mother Hardey at St. Michael were: Susannah Boudreau, who founded the first house of the Society in New Zealand in 1880; Margaret Gallwey and Rose Gauthreaux, who both became vice-vicars of the West; Mary Frances Peacock, who helped to found the convent at Halifax; and Ellen Jennings, who headed the first convent of the Sacred Heart in Albany, New York.

with which you deal with me," Mother Barat wrote (January 9, 1838), and later, after the trouble with Bishop Blanc:

> Divine Providence allowed all these difficulties to test us...to attach me more to you and your house. You are the Sacred Heart's and my first American daughter. That is enough. Besides, naturally I love your country and its fine qualities. We shall always get along well together. So do not worry about what you hear; none of this gossip makes the slightest impression on me. I shall turn to you for clarification and remain at peace (February 26, 1838).

That same year, Mother Barat had expressed her pleasure at Mother Hardey's handling of authority: "I like your style of government. It seems to me to come from God" (January 9, 1838). The same year, Mother Barat twice wrote of her desire for strong union in the Society between the Old World and the New, asking that two talented novices from America be sent to the French novitiate so that "the already intimate bonds that unite us will become still stronger and so will perpetuate our spirit, which ought to be the same everywhere should we become worldwide."[25]

She realized that the needs of America would require adaptations, but the spirit must be the same: "I desire so ardently that the Society will strengthen itself in America, that it will be founded on true religious spirit, a spirit that will not frighten others" (March 1, 1840). Mother Hardey learned that spirit first from Mother Audé at Grand Coteau and St. Michael, and through many adaptations,

---

25 Through the following years, a number of American novices and aspirants were sent by Mother Hardey in response, to Conflans and other French houses. Mother Barat was not always impressed by the selection.

she kept it intact. Mother Barat counted on her to do so: "You are first in my thought," she wrote in 1840.

NEW DECREES

In 1839, controversial new decrees were adopted by the General Council. They threatened to divide the Society, so strongly were they opposed by many. In faraway America, Mother Hardey tried loyally to accept them: "It has always seemed to me that nothing could be more perfect than our *Constitutions*, that it would be impossible to improve them, but now I see that the changes which have been made are exactly what was needed."[26]

Mother Barat was pleased with her haste to obey, "What consolation you have given me by your submission to receive and practice the Decrees!"[27] She had Mother Hardey's letter inserted in the *Lettres annuelles* of 1839, adding a tribute to the convent of St. Michael. Mother Elisabeth Galitzine had been sent to America to present the decrees, and Mother Barat advised Mother Hardey to strive to enter fully into her views. At the same time, she told her to make known the customs in use, and the inconveniences that might arise from adopting the decrees. What Mother Hardey did not know at that time was that Mother Barat herself was ambiguous about the decrees and the changes they would bring, but in her patient wisdom, was allowing their advocates to try them experimentally.[28]

---

26 Williams, *Second Sowing*, 151-152, quote with no source given.

27 Mother Barat to Mother Hardey, May 14, 1840.

28 For an account of the complex relationships that followed, see Jeanne de Charry, RSCJ, *The Canonical and Legal Evolution of the Society of the Sacred Heart of Jesus from 1827 to 1853* (Rome, 1991), pp. 4-15.

Mother Galitzine, a Russian princess raised in the Russian Orthodox Church, now an assistant general of the Society, aroused curious interest wherever she went in America. Mother Hardey dreaded the ordeal of meeting her, even as the representative of Mother Barat. But Mother Galitzine's simple manner dispelled fear. Mother Hardey liked her frankness and initially was won by her single-minded sincerity. Only later did she realize and suffer for many years from the results of Mother Galitzine's impetuous action and lack of wisdom.[29] It was left for Mother Hardey to reverse Mother Galitzine's decisions. She had to move the novitiate from McSherrystown, Pennsylvania, where Mother Galitzine had established it, because of continuing fatal cases of tuberculosis there. Mother Galitzine had determined the closing of St. Charles, almost breaking the heart of the valiant Mother Duchesne, but Mother Hardey urged that it be retained as a day school, and Mother Barat agreed with her. Meanwhile, Mother Galitzine was planning a foundation in New York and needed Mother Hardey to help her.

---

29 For example, In New York, Mother Galitzine unknowingly incurred a large debt for the Society. Unidentified boxes of vestments and other things arrived at the New York convent from Europe. She assumed they were gifts for the "American missions," and Mother Hardey was told to dispose of them at once, though she urged delay. Finally, M. Montravel came to claim his property, and Mother Hardey was left to pay their value of 10,000 francs. This required years and was a constant reminder to her of Mother Galitzine's imprudent action.

Aloysia Hardey to Mother Barat, 23 January 1843. In it, among other things, she expresses the confusion of the RSCJ in America about the new decrees of 1839.

3

NEW YORK AND FRANCE

NEW YORK

In 1841, Mother Hardey was called to New York to join Mother Galitzine and the group of founders opening a convent there. Traveling a week by way of Cincinnati and Philadelphia, by stagecoach and steamboat, they reached New York on May 17. Bishop John Hughes[30] had selected a house on Houston Street for them, a former school, now become a boarding house whose landlady continued to rent out rooms even after Mother Hardey and a few religious took possession of the empty ones. As the guests vacated a room, the religious would occupy and clean it, until finally it became their own. On June 3, Mother Galitzine and the other religious left the hospitality of the Sisters of Charity to be with those who had already moved in. The new school grew under Mother Hardey's care, and Mother Galitzine had an opportunity to form an opinion of her gifts.[31]

---

30 John Hughes (1797-1864), born in Ireland, emigrated to the U.S. in 1817, was ordained in 1826, and was bishop and archbishop of New York 1842-1864, a time of tremendous growth in the church there.

31 The first pupil of the New York house was Margaret Dunne, who was accepted *gratis*. Born in Brooklyn in 1829, she later became a Religious of the Sacred Heart. Pro-

Houston St., 1841, first foundation in New York.

In 1842 Mother Hardey was chosen to accompany Mother Galitzine to the General Council that would end the three years of experimentation with the decrees of 1839. Mother Barat wrote earnestly to Mother Hardey: "Hold fast to the trunk of the tree no matter what you may hear! Make known to me your doubts, your uneasiness, for we shall always understand each other." She repeated her desire to visit America: "I would like so much to see you and stay with you a few months. But I can no longer hope to make the journey. I am too old. However, I want to know my first American daughter."[32]

Mother Hardey looked forward with keen anticipation to meeting Mother Barat, and she had hopes of seeing Mother Audé once again.

---

fessed at Manhattanville in 1850, she went on to be a founder in Omaha and died at Kenwood in 1893.

32 Letters of May 16, 1839; June 15, 1841.

FRANCE

Mother Hardey was free to sail for France in the spring when Mother Bathilde Sallion arrived in New York to take charge of the school in her absence.[33] She was not to see Mother Audé again, as news of her death arrived shortly before their departure. But at last, she would meet Mother Barat. It was at Lyons that the travelers found her, for she had gone to that city to convene the Council. Mother Hardey was struck with shyness as she was introduced to Mother Barat, who greeted her lovingly, exclaiming as she embraced the thirty-one-year-old, so soon to be charged with all the American houses, "She is very young!"[34]

Though most of the superiors of the Society had arrived in Lyons for the Council, Archbishop Denys Affre of Paris forbade it to be convened. The situation was one of political and ecclesiastical complexity, but an element causing the prohibition was probably the fear that the Council might carry out the decision already made in 1839 to move the motherhouse of the Society from his city to Rome. So there was no Council, but Mother Barat asked Father Joseph Barelle, S.J., to preach a retreat on the interior life for the assembled councilors. She said of it later: "I have never heard a retreat like it. We felt that a special communication of light and grace had been given by God in these pressing needs of the Society."[35]

---

33 In December 1842, Mother Sallion went to Canada to make the foundation of St. Jacques de l'Achigan. Mother Galitzine had visited the place in September of the previous year, and neither she nor Mother Hardey realized what travel to Canada in the winter would entail, both in danger and suffering. Bathilde Sallion, RSCJ (1791-1875) entered the Society in Paris in 1828, came to America in 1841, and was treasurer of many of the American houses before returning to France in 1852.

34 *Vie*, p. 91.

35 Baunard, 137.

Its theme impressed Mother Hardey profoundly, and it represented a turning point in her spiritual life. Never before in her years of full activity had there been such a time set apart for reflection and deepening of prayer. Now at Lyons, she made up for the lack of a "traditional" novitiate and probation, which usually provided months of prayerful reflection removed from ordinary activity. Here she had Mother Barat to counsel her. On her return to New York, however, Mother Hardey was to feel more keenly than ever the lack of spiritual direction. She missed Mother Barat: "Letters are a century in coming," she wrote.[36]

Bishop Hughes' advice had always been, "Do what common sense tells you." But Father Barelle was adding another dimension when he wrote: "Pray, reflect, then act for God and his glory," and later: "Let yourself be led from within by the Spirit of Our Lord." It was this message of interior life that she in turn was to hand on to her communities.

---

[36] January 23, 1843. She was probably not aware that the turnaround time had shortened significantly from the six months in the early years of Philippine, only one or two months at this point between Paris and New York.

4

RESPONSIBILITY

VISITATOR

Before the aborted Council of 1842, Mother Galitzine was suggesting Mother Hardey as a replacement for herself as provincial.[37] She wrote to Mother Barat: "If you name her provincial on her return to America, the nomination will be favorably received in all our houses. Our communities have the highest idea of her merit—she enjoys universal esteem." Mother Duchesne's esteem was to be valued above all others: "Mother Hardey would be my choice," she wrote, suggesting to Mother Boilvin: "It would give greater satisfaction generally both outside the convents and within, if we had a provincial who was an American by birth and language."[38]

Consequently, when Mother Galitzine died of yellow fever at St. Michael in December 1843, Mother Hardey was named visitator (official representative of the superior general) and charged

---

37 The office of provincial was one of the innovations of the new decrees of 1839 that did not last after their revocation. Instead, superiors vicar were instituted in 1851 and remained in place until 1967-1970.

38 Philippine Duchesne to Adeline Boilvin, RSCJ, January 6, 1844.

with all the American houses. The following year she shared her responsibilities with Mother Maria Cutts, who became visitor of the West, while she retained jurisdiction over the convents of the Eastern United States and Canada. Again in 1872, she would be named visitor of the North American houses before going to Paris as assistant general.

DANGER

1844 was the year of the Nativist American persecution of Catholics. There was destruction of life and property in Philadelphia; there were riots in New York. In a lively letter from New York, Mother Hardey describes to Mother Barat

> the horrible events which occurred in Philadelphia and which people feared and still fear may be renewed in this city. I mean the almost general massacre of Catholics and destruction of churches. Priests were forced into disguise and fled....All the churches were closed or used by the soldiers, for the city is under martial law.

She describes the single wall of the Augustinian Church still standing with its inscription, "God sees you," then continues:

> Peace has been restored ...fears are now entertained for our city. Several parents withdrew their children; others left them to assure our safety. For several nights we kept ourselves in readiness to leave the house in case of attack, but so far, the excitement has not broken out

into violence. It is the general opinion that danger to us arises only from our proximity to the Cathedral.... I have not had a moment of fear....during those nights when we were apparently awaiting death, I had not the least dread of it. Why?[39]

ASTORIA

The danger of more rioting may have prompted the swift removal of the school on Houston Street to a country property in Astoria. In any case, Ravenswood, "the nicest little property five miles from New York," opened on September 12, 1844. The new location was attractive, fronting the East River, but it proved somewhat inaccessible, and in three years the house became too small for the ever-increasing numbers of pupils and novices.

MANHATTANVILLE

The desirable Lorillard estate in Manhattanville was up for sale. Bishop Hughes on a visit to Paris in 1846 persuaded Mother Barat of the wisdom of still another move for the New York house. On the very day of his return from Europe he brought to Mother Hardey in person the news of her approval. So the property was purchased after the price was reduced through the novena of prayer of the religious and students, and one member of the Lorillard family opposing the sale had died suddenly. Bishop Hughes commented, "Be careful not to oppose Mother Hardey's wishes, for if necessary, she will kill you with her novenas.[40] The

---

39 To Mother Barat, May 15, 1844.
40 Williams, *Second Sowing*, p. 240.

Manhattanville, New York, 1847

convent of the Sacred Heart was moved at once to Manhattanville. It remained there for over a century.

With the new responsibilities of visitor, Mother Hardey retained the charge of mistress general of the boarding school at Manhattanville and followed every detail of school life. The enrollment continued to grow as the excellence of the school became known; in ten years it had reached two hundred. In America some modification of the rule for French boarding schools was necessary. Parents were allowed to visit more frequently, and to take their daughters out with them once a month. But every change that was made drew criticism. There was criticism of the more democratic "mix" in the schools;[41] criticism of the worldliness of some of the former pupils of Astoria; criticism of the secular attire worn by Mother Hardey when she traveled from Manhattanville to the day school now opened on Bleecker Street.

---

41 A letter of January 26, 1846, explains to Mother Barat the absence of class distinction in America, something she had been hearing from Philippine from the beginning of the mission.

Some were shocked at her means of transportation. She was too poor to own a carriage or even pay fare on an omnibus, so she often rode in a butcher's cart, or beside a farmer bringing his produce downtown.[42] Having explained her actions to Mother Barat, she would smile at such criticism and continue her travels for the glory of the Sacred Heart.

RUMORS

Shortly after the move to Manhattanville, Mother Hardey fitted out one of the buildings for a parish school, though as yet there was no parish. Later, at Bishop Hughes's request, she agreed to care for a group of orphans, while the Sisters of Charity, whose usual work it was, were unable to take them. As this was not the customary work of the Society, it also aroused criticism. At this time the Sisters of Charity of New York had separated from the group at Emmitsburg who had joined the French Daughters of Charity, thus creating an American branch. Rumor began to spread that Mother Hardey was planning to do the same with the Society of the Sacred Heart. It was a rumor completely unfounded and was a source of great pain to Mother Hardey. Her prime objective from the earliest days of her religious life had been to keep a close union between the American convents and the motherhouse in Paris. This was well known to Mother Barat who wrote consoling her: "I know you through and through, and what I am convinced of above all is your sincere attachment to the Society. As for the rest, you know that people are not perfect, and that we must all make allowances for one

---

42 Mother Hardey said: "With my veil over my face I can pass as the farmer's wife." Williams, p. 269.

another."⁴³ That anyone could suspect her of separating from the motherhouse was one of the greatest sufferings of her life, Mother Hardey admitted later.

When the move from Astoria to Manhattanville was completed in February 1847, two more houses were opened and more requests for foundations accepted. In March the religious in Philadelphia moved outside the city to the new property of Eden Hall. In Canada, Saint-Vincent, near Montreal, was opened as a boarding school. There were requests for foundations by Bishop William Walsh of Halifax when he visited in October, and by Bishop John McCloskey of Albany when he came to Manhattanville in November.⁴⁴ Mother Hardey could not refuse. Understandably, she wrote to Mother Barat, "I cannot do all I wish in spite of rising at 4:00. There are a thousand things that suffer."⁴⁵ Mother Barat did what she could to send her help. "You are first in my thought," she had written. Now she wrote: "If I were younger and could endure a long trip, I would rush to see you and all our very dear American houses. Useless desire; only in heaven will we be together."⁴⁶

But she was able to send as mistress of novices, Mother Marie Thérèse Trincano to relieve Mother Hardey at least of that charge. This gifted religious was to become her loyal friend and trusted support, her "second self," on whose help she could count for the foundations that lay ahead, in Buffalo, Detroit, and Canada.

---

43 January 31, 1853.

44 William Walsh (1804-1858) attended Maynooth seminary in Ireland and was ordained there in 1828. He was the first bishop and later archbishop of Halifax when the diocese of Nova Scotia was divided in two in 1844. John McCloskey (1810-1885) was bishop of Albany 1847-1864, then succeeded Archbishop Hughes as the first American-born archbishop of New York in 1864.

45 April 6, 1847.

46 March 1, 1840, and April 27, 1847.

REFUGEES

Europe was torn by revolutions in 1848. Anti-Catholic governments drove the Religious of the Sacred Heart from Italy and Switzerland. Violence in France threatened the motherhouse in Paris. Mother Hardey offered Mother Barat a place of refuge in New York, praying that the Heart of Jesus would "bring her here" where she would be "perfectly at peace." She expressed the hope that more refugees would come to America, advising that the religious travel in secular dress, using the title Mrs. or Miss. She longed especially for rapid communication, a "transoceanic telegraph" to keep her informed. Mother Hardey would have delighted in the instant electronic contacts of the twentieth century.

5

FOUNDATIONS

FOUNDATIONS

As the threat to Paris passed and the revolutions subsided in Europe, Mother Hardey's anxiety gave way to intense labor as she arranged for the foundation of six convents in as many years. This meant a sacrifice of personnel for Manhattanville, and a still heavier schedule of planning and travel for her. It was a distressing time, a period of uncontrolled epidemics of cholera and fevers in many American cities, and several of the newly founded convents were affected.

In 1849, Mother Hardey accompanied the founders to Halifax on their three-day boat trip from New York.[47] Founded the same year, the Buffalo convent suffered more than any other in the cholera epidemic of 1852, which claimed the lives of four religious

---

47 When in 1850 an epidemic of scarlet fever forced Mother Mary Frances Peacock to move the Halifax convent without waiting for her approval, Mother Hardey commended her for acting swiftly in this emergency. She herself had been given wide freedom of action by Mother Barat (Garvey, p. 139). Mother Peacock was the sister of Mrs. Cornelia Connelly, who had lived with her family at Grand Coteau when Mother Hardey was in Louisiana. When Mrs. Connelly was trying her vocation to religious life at the Trinità dei Monti in Rome, Mother Hardey advised Mother Barat: "Mrs. Connelly is better fitted to found a new order, than to enter an existing one." Later, she founded the Society of the Holy Child Jesus (Williams, *Second Sowing*, p. 308).

Halifax, Nova Scotia, 1849

and left great poverty in its wake.[48] Three years later, the illfated academy was moved to Rochester where it flourished for over a hundred years. The Detroit house, also founded in 1849, met with legal and episcopal problems. The religious moved four times before they were settled in 1856.[49] The house in Albany, founded in 1852, also moved to another location until in 1859, the beautiful Rathbone estate of Kenwood was purchased. Mother Hardey had great hopes for Kenwood, and a few years later she was planning for a new building spacious enough to accommodate the New

---

48 The visits of Mother Hardey with their financial help and spiritual inspiration "lifted us to new courage," the annalist notes in the house journal of Buffalo. Both she and Mother du Rousier visited the stricken convent during the cholera epidemic.

49 The Detroit foundation was not settled for ten years. The Beaubien heirs contested in court the donation of the land to the convent. A condition of this donation was that the religious care for a group of orphans. They needed an academy to support the orphans, but Bishop Peter Lefèvre wanted a free school, not an academy. In an attempt to gain his goal, he deprived the convent of Mass and the reservation of the Blessed Sacrament. Only a letter from Mother Barat in Paris achieved a reconciliation. The orphans were transferred to a new convent across the river in Sandwich, Ontario. A free school was built near the academy on Jefferson Avenue in Detroit. In 1859, the Sandwich convent was moved to London, Ontario.

York novitiate and a large boarding school. Meanwhile, the new wing and chapel at Manhattanville were completed in 1850, and the chapel at Eden Hall was dedicated in 1851. Mother Trincano felt that the special blessing of God was upon Mother Hardey's work when she wrote to Mother Barat in September 1851: "God blesses Mother Hardey's work in a special way; her charity, her spirit of prayer, all the virtues of which she gives us the example must necessarily draw the blessing of the Heart of Jesus."

After the General Council of 1851, which created the office of superior vicar, Mother Hardey's title became that of vice-vicar of the Eastern United States and Canada, but she retained the offices at Manhattanville of superior, mistress general, treasurer, and once more, mistress of novices. When Mother Margaret Donnelly died, she had to replace her teaching a class as well. It was in vain that Mother Barat urged that she divide her work. There was no one else to do it.

MOTHER ANA DU ROUSIER

After the Council of 1851, Mother Ana du Rousier was sent as vicar to visit the houses of North America, and to report to Mother Barat.[50] She found Manhattanville beautifully located. "It would do us honor even in France," she wrote to Mother

---

50 Mother Barat may have felt that a mission in the New World was what Mother du Rousier needed at that time. She had enjoyed great success as provincial of Turin until a revolution overthrew the monarchy. She then suffered calumny and persecution, forced to flee with the rest of the Religious of the Sacred Heart. In Paris during the next few years, she met with failure as mistress general of the Rue de Varennes. Mother Barat wrote to Mother Hardey as Mother du Rousier was beginning her visitation, no doubt anticipating some tension between them: "I cannot repeat too much the advice I gave you on leaving, to be one with your Mother Vicar, to be at ease with her, and to give her your complete confidence; trust that the greatest good and prosperity of your houses will be the result." (June 29, 1852)

Barat. But the little houses of Albany and Buffalo must have been a surprising contrast to the convents in Paris.

Her report to Mother Barat was not entirely favorable. She judged the religious reserved; only those from France were open and frank with her, helped no doubt by the ability to communicate with her in her own language. She found fault with Mother Hardey's government and formation of the young sisters; she objected to her holding so many offices; she disapproved of the concentration of houses in New York State. By January 1853, her public complaints were causing such suffering to Mother Hardey that Mother Barat wrote to encourage and console her. In New York, Mother Hardey and Mother du Rousier must have presented a contrast: Mother Hardey, tall, attractive in appearance, a "charmer" as her earliest biographer states; Mother du Rousier, small, slightly deformed with one shoulder noticeably higher than the other, requiring an interpreter in all her dealings with Americans. Mother Hardey appreciated the difficulty of Mother du Rousier's situation: "Her devotedness to our mission is as great as her position is difficult." Temperamentally they were probably incompatible, as subsequent letters suggest. It was difficult for both of them. But Mother du Rousier remained only a year, before continuing on to Chile to establish the Society of the Sacred Heart in South America.[51]

---

51 *Vie*, p.78. November 14, 1856. Mother Hardey's letter to Mother Adèle Cahier, secretary general, expresses her frustration at having to submit major decisions to Mother du Rousier who was residing in Chile: "Why don't you put off the decision regarding these foundations until after the next Council; if Mother du Rousier does not return, then surely we will have some other Mother Vicar, and that will be satisfactory in every way." She herself became Vicar after the Council of 1864.

WEARINESS

Meanwhile, financial affairs required Mother Hardey's time and attention as the tempo of life and work increased in 1854. She was feeling the burden of responsibility as never before, as well as the pain of separation from trusted friends. She was now forty-five. It was a time of intense weariness of body and soul. When Mother Amélie Jouve was sent to Louisiana as vice-vicar, Mother Hardey complained to Mother Barat on March 24, 1855, that she had taken her "one, only, intimate friend, the person of whom I could ask secret advice." In 1856, another friend, her Assistant Mother Trincano, was sent to Canada as superior. Some of the religious caused her pain.[52] Her own sister Mathilde was dissatisfied with every assignment given her and finally left the Society.[53]

Foundations continued. After a cholera epidemic in St. John, New Brunswick, Mother Hardey opened a convent to care for the orphans. In 1856, she transferred the boarding school from Saint-Vincent still closer to Montreal, to the Sault-au-Récollet. In New York, she built a handsome brownstone "Gothic house" on 17th Street for the day school. "The house is the most religious I know in America," she wrote, a single building for academy and free school, with both rich and poor under one roof.[54] Neigh-

---

52 Mother Hardey wrote of one person whom she had not known personally before. "She is not as difficult nearby, as I had thought." Of another she wrote: "She is the most difficult and trying saint that I have seen. She will make us saints; that is the essential." This referred to Stanislas Tommasini (Hardey to Mother Barat, April 4, 1855).

53 Mathilde Hardey was born in 1813 in Maryland and moved with the family to Louisiana, where she entered the Society at St. Michael in1829. She was professed there years later and served in a number of houses before leaving the Society from Rochester in 1864.

54 When more space was needed for the parish school in 1867, Mother Hardey used some of the funds she had reserved for completing Kenwood to erect a school building

Pensionnat du Sacré-Cœur Sault-au-Récollet (P. Q.)

Convent of the Sacred Heart Sault-au-Récollet

Sault-au-Récollet, Montreal, 1856

bors who had opposed having a convent in the area congratulated the religious on the fine school. One request for a foundation at that time, however, had to be refused: that of Sacramento, California, though Mother Hardey favored accepting the offer of land for a school.[55]

CUBA

Still another foundation was made in the same decade, that of Havana, Cuba.[56] It nearly cost Mother Hardey her life. Mother

---

on 17th Street (March 24, 1855).

55 Mother Hardey wrote to Mother Barat: "Since the railroad is finished, and the Isthmus may be crossed in four hours instead of three days, as when Mother Vicar went to Chile, I feel that we are wrong in refusing a most favorable position, especially since the Archbishop only asks a promise to go there" (March 24, 1855).

56 Mother Hardey saw the possibilities of Cuba as a health resort: "The location will be desirable also for people with lung trouble. Many New Yorkers prolong their lives by staying in Havana for several months" (October 19, 1856). A strange contradiction to the fear of pervasive yellow fever.

Barat had been reluctant to open a house on the island. She wrote on November 9, 1857: "I am told that foreigners are especially liable to take yellow fever which annually visits the island....It is with trembling heart that I say to you, 'Go, my dearest Aloysia!'" Her premonition was to prove correct. Mother Hardey was accompanied on this journey by Mother Stanislas Tommasini, who served as companion and interpreter.[57] Mother Hardey made new friends, found a suitable house, sparked a fund-raising effort, placed the school on a firm financial basis, then succumbed to a nearly fatal attack of yellow fever. It was three months before she could return to New York, arriving, however, almost before the news of her illness reached Manhattanville.

EXCEPTION

When a request for missionaries for Chile reached New York, Mother Hardey volunteered to go. Usually calm Mother Trincano was so upset by this that she spoke of it to Bishop Hughes. The thought of Mother Hardey leaving New York prompted the Bishop to write at once to Mother Barat in Paris, listing five cogent reasons why she should remain, and begging a dispensation from any rule requiring a change of superiors. Blending gentle strength and tact, Mother Barat replied in January 1859:

---

[57] Maria Luigia Angelica Cipriana Stanislas Tommasini, born in Parma in 1827, came to New York when her house in Pignerol was closed by the revolution of 1848. She taught Spanish and Italian at Manhattanville for twenty-three years, and was later superior in Havana, vicar in Canada, superior and mistress of novices at the trilingual novitiate in Grand Coteau, and one of the founders in Mexico in 1883. She died at Kenwood in 1913.

El Cerro, Havana, 1858

It is impossible for me to understand how you could have been informed of a project which I have not entertained...There is no rule without an exception... A thousand motives authorize this one, on account of the peculiar position in which our houses in America are placed. I know well the capabilities and devotedness, as well as the virtues of our good Mother Hardey. No one can appreciate them more than myself.

So Mother Hardey remained in New York, leaving only after the death of both Mother Barat and Bishop Hughes.

PARIS

The expectation of all was that the General Council would meet in the fall of 1860. So that summer, when Mother Amélie Jouve, vice-vicar of the West, received word while visiting Mother Hardey in New York to hurry to Paris, Mother Hardey took for granted that she too was to leave a few months early to attend. Only on her arrival in Paris did she discover that this was not the case. There was no shadow, however, on the welcome she received, and for several weeks in her contacts with Mother Barat, she drew strength and courage for the suffering that lay ahead.

6

ILLNESS AND CIVIL WAR

ILLNESS

A series of tragic events occurred at Manhattanville during the winter of 1861. One of the pupils died; an accident to a workman doing construction work resulted in his death; a fire started one night in the laundry next to the house. Though she was ill, Mother Hardey saw to the safety of all during the night of the fire, with the result that her condition became grave. A stroke paralyzed her right arm, preventing her from using her hand to write for the rest of her life. This was to be a profound and constant suffering for her, though she accepted it fully. "God wills it," she said.

She had carried on an extensive correspondence; now she was dependent on a secretary to convey her thoughts and wishes in writing. Mother Barat better than anyone understood the depths of her pain. Anxious to know the extent of the paralysis, she wrote, "If you can, my daughter, add a few lines in your own hand to reassure me." Shortly after, she begged Mother Hardey to take care of herself, adding, "After seeing your writing, though it is much changed, my poor heart can breathe again." The few lines Mother Hardey sent to Mother Barat were the last she ever wrote herself.

Mother Margaret Hoey stepped in as her secretary for the next fourteen years.

Mother Hardey went to Kenwood to recuperate. The preceding fall she had announced the opening of a normal school for teacher training at Manhattanville, but her own illness and that of Mother Peacock who was to direct it prevented action on the project.[58] Her foundations continued, however. She planned for a day school on Beaver Street in Albany and accepted the offer of Bishop Ignatius Bourget of a house in Montreal for a day school and a meeting place for alumnae in the city. Soon there were retreats for "ladies of the world," and by 1861, a sewing circle of the Children of Mary.[59]

CIVIL WAR

In the spring of 1861, civil war broke out in the United States between North and South. It must have been an agony for her to find her Southern homeland regarded as enemy territory. Her own suffering served to increase her compassion for that of others, and she worked with her usual energy to alleviate it. In April, she wrote to Mother Barat describing the "sad condition of our poor states." Communications were cut between North and South. There was fighting only a day's journey from New York. All 200,000 troops passed through New York on their way to help the capital. Food was beyond price. "How can we live if this state of things continues?" she asked on April 20, 1861.

---

58 The normal school was to begin with a dozen graduates of the parish school at Manhattanville, and Mother Peacock was to organize this work.

59 Mother Barat had left the decision about Montreal to her, all the while writing in her letter of April 28, 1861, about how much good could be done there where most of the population was, in distinction from the country where the Sault was located.

As schools in Washington and Georgetown closed, Mother Hardey offered Manhattanville as a place of refuge for the Visitation nuns in case of evacuation, but this did not occur. At Manhattanville no pupils were withdrawn, but many parents, especially from the South, were unable to pay for their daughters' education. One Southerner attending the school during the war wrote of Mother Hardey's kindness, "Received as a *gratis* pupil, a little Rebel refugee, never shall I forget her delicate generosity."[60]

Fathers of some of the Manhattanville pupils were generals of the occupation forces in Louisiana. Through their friendship with Mother Hardey, provisions and security were provided for the convent of Grand Coteau. A letter to the superior, Mother Amélie Jouve, from General Nathaniel P. Banks is indicative of their concern and kindness toward the community and pupils:

> If you desire to send letters to New York, you will please forward them to me by the bearer who is instructed to wait for them. I send a safeguard that will protect your school from the struggle in the rear of my column, and if you desire it, will leave a guard. My daughter is with Madame Hardey in New York. I have ordered the Commissary in Chief to forward to your Order at the Convent small quantities of flour, coffee, tea, fine salt and other articles that may be useful—which I beg you will accept—if you get them—with my regards.[61]

---

60 Williams, *Second Sowing*, p. 367.

61 April 20, 1863. Callan, *Society*, pp. 526-29. Original correspondence, Provincial Archives, St. Louis, Missouri.

The "small quantities" proved to be: 100 pounds of coffee; five barrels of meal; two barrels of flour; one half chest of tea; one barrel of sugar, and five bags of salt. Through their contacts with Mother Hardey, both he and Major General Benjamin Butler aided Mother Anna Shannon to travel across the lines of occupation to visit the other convents in Louisiana.

TRAVEL

For eighteen months there had been no communication between the convents of Missouri and Louisiana, so at Mother Barat's request, in August 1862, Mother Hardey visited the Western houses, with which she was charged while the war situation remained. The demands on her charity were many that year, but she managed to give financial assistance to Chile, as well as to St. Louis and St. Joseph. On the way to St. Louis, she visited the Chicago house, founded from there only three years before. Everywhere she was received with joy as the envoy of Mother Barat. Her words of encouragement and generous aid were welcomed with gratitude. Travel under war conditions was slow and difficult, and Mother Hardey was in poor health. Mother Barat expressed her concern and appreciation: "How I suffered on learning of the feeble state of your health. Our Lord knows that it has been shattered by the labors undergone for the welfare of his little Society. He will not forget your self-sacrifice."[62]

But by the following winter, Mother Hardey was traveling again. In 1863, she opened a second house in Cuba, Santo Spiritu. Though it promised well, war in Cuba forced its closing after five years. While Mother Hardey was there, she learned that her father

---
62 Garvey, p. 251.

had died in Louisiana three months before.[63] Typically, she kept the news of her sorrow to herself, unwilling to cast a cloud over the joy of the foundation.

CHANGES

In 1864, Bishop Hughes died. It was a great loss for the Society, whose friend and defender he had been since the first days in New York. He had held Mother Hardey in the highest esteem.[64] He was succeeded by another friend from the early days at Houston Street, Bishop John McCloskey, who had been chaplain there, and later had helped the religious in Astoria and Albany. He was to remain close to the Society when he became Cardinal Archbishop of New York.

The year also ushered in change in the government of the Society in America. The last General Council over which Mother Barat presided relieved Mother Hardey of some of her burden, leaving in her vicariate only the eight houses of the Eastern United States and Cuba. Canada became a separate vicariate; the South and West were to be vice-vicariates. Mother Barat wrote that she expected Mother Hardey to lend the help of "her experience and devotedness" to the convents of Missouri, and that Mother Gallwey would be "charged temporarily with Missouri and the Potawatomi (the Indian Mission) with the

---

63 The news of her father's death three months earlier had come from the South by way of Canada, as there was no communication with the North.

64 July 16, 1861. Even as he dismisses some complaints "whose source" he knew, as "false and malicious," Bishop Hughes writes to Cardinal Barnaba expressing his high opinion of Mother Hardey: "I do not believe that there is a religious in this country more above suspicion than Mother Hardey of the Sacred Heart, as there is perhaps hardly another who in the sphere of her vocation has accomplished more good. But the purest and the best cannot always escape."

advice of Mother Hardey.[65] The separation of the Canadian Vicariate was painful to all. In the *Lettres annuelles,* the religious of Halifax mentioned the sacrifice entailed as "most of us since the beginning of our religious life have known no other government than that of our reverend and very kind Mother Hardey." The religious of the London (Ontario) house expressed their gratitude, "She has overwhelmed us with kindness." But a note of hope was struck in the comments in the house journal of Montreal: "Building projects give us hope of seeing again in Canada this beloved Mother, so worthy of our affection and of our profound esteem, still more of our eternal gratitude."

The United States Civil War finally came to an end as Mother Hardey was returning from Cuba before the Easter of 1865. But the assassination of President Lincoln continued the national mourning. The Easter vacation at Manhattanville was prolonged. Feelings ran high among both Northern and Southern pupils. When they returned to school, they were forbidden to wear mourning badges to class. It required Mother Hardey's utmost skill to keep the large boarding school functioning calmly, and to avoid division.[66]

---

65 Mother Barat to the houses of America, August 25, 1864.

66 The daughter of the Northern activist Horace Greeley was in the school at the time. Earlier crises had been averted by Mother Hardey's tact. On one occasion when the refugee Bishop Labastida, exiled from Mexico by President Comonfort, was living at Manhattanville, the President's daughter, a pupil there, brought her father to a Mass celebrated by the bishop. Fortunately, no unpleasant incident occurred. Later, when he was reinstated in his country, the bishop repaid Mother Hardey's hospitality by inviting the Society of the Sacred Heart to found a house in Mexico.

7

MORE CHANGES

MOTHER BARAT'S DEATH

Mourning continued and intensified that spring when news of Mother Barat's death on May 25 reached the convents of America. For all, it was a deep personal grief, but perhaps no one suffered her loss more keenly than Mother Hardey. For thirty years by letter and personal contact Mother Barat had trained and advised and fostered the spiritual growth of her "first American daughter." Mother Hardey had received from her the vision of what the Society of the Sacred Heart should be in America and had striven tirelessly and with her whole heart to make that vision a reality. In the first flush of sorrow, she wrote to Mother Josephine Gœtz on June 13 that though time might lessen the bitterness:

> It will never efface from my heart the remembrance of one who was everything to me. Her example, her words, the advice she so often gave will remain graven in my soul, and the study of my life will be always to merit that from heaven she still looks at me with a loving smile.

Kenwood, Albany, New York, 1870

Mother Hardey continued to spend her energies to the full "to make her spirit live" in the Society in America.

KENWOOD

The following year, 1866, Manhattanville finally made the sacrifice of Mother Hardey, whose presence was needed in Albany. In September she wrote that for her the sacrifice was "bitter to the heart," but sweetened by the thought that she was obeying. After twenty-five years in New York, it was hard to leave. Once at Kenwood, Mother Hardey set about the erection of an imposing building on the terraced hillside where the Rathbone mansion had stood. She followed the details of construction in person. Whether she was home, or traveling in the United States or Cuba, she insisted on having "regular information of the *daily* progress" of the work.[67] Its completion was delayed until 1871, as she was asked by Mother Gœtz, now superior general, to send funds reserved for that purpose to St. Louis, where the Maryville convent was in process of construction. A convent, noviciate and boarding school, Kenwood was the culmination of Mother Hardey's long career of building for the glory of the Heart of Jesus.

THE WEST

In 1869, after attending to the business needs of St. Louis, Mother Hardey traveled on to St. Mary's, Kansas, the Indian mission of the Potawatomi. Since the Indians were moving away, there was question of suppressing the school. Instead, Mother Hardey decided to build a new one for the children of the white settlers who replaced them. Hers was the delicate task of separating the funds of the Society of the Sacred Heart from those of the Society of Jesus, for since 1841 until this time the religious and the Jesuit missionaries had owned and administered them jointly. The division was worked out and a separate corporation set up for the academy. Bishop Jean-Baptiste Miège of Leavenworth, who witnessed the transaction, was deeply impressed by Mother Hardey's business acumen and by her character, that of "a finished type" of Religious of the Sacred Heart.[68]

Mother Hardey left for a retreat in Paris in the summer of 1869. On the whole, it was a restful time until Mother Gœtz suggested that she might be named assistant general in the future. So, after her return to America there was increased urgency in

---

67 Mother Sarah Jones in correspondence with Mother Margaret Hoey, July 26, 1866.
68 Garvey, p. 294.

her work. She made the long-desired foundation of Cincinnati, Ohio, promised for thirty-five years, and that of Rosecroft, Maryland. Rosecroft was especially loved by Mother Hardey. It was donated to the Society by her stepmother, whose home it had been, and whose daughter Lena[69] was entering as a novice.[70] It was beautifully located, and prospered in many ways, but in a few years its relative isolation and consequent lack of spiritual help forced its closing.

FRANCE 1870

Mother Hardey took up her residence once more at Manhattanville as political trouble was again erupting in France. It was the year of the Franco-Prussian War and the Paris Commune. In Paris, as street fighting threatened the safety of the motherhouse, Mother Hardey was swift to offer hospitality to any religious forced to flee.[71] An evacuation was not needed, however, but financial assistance was, and Mother Hardey, with her usual generosity, sent all she could spare.

---

69 Lena Hardey, Aloysia's half-sister, was born in 1852, entered the Society, and died as a novice in 1876.

70 Garvey, p.305-306. She wrote to Mother Gœtz: "The property is beautifully situated on the St. Mary's River, one hundred and twenty miles from Baltimore, and consists of 300 acres...As it is almost surrounded by water, the place offers all the advantages of sea-bathing which would be very beneficial to our invalids; and there is always abundance of fish and oysters, and I may add that this place is regarded as the cradle of Catholicity in Maryland, as the first Catholic colony landed here in 1634."

71 Marie Dufour, *Vie de la très Révérende Mère Marie-Joséphine Gœtz*, pp. 378-79. In Halifax, the bishop and Religious of the Sacred Heart invited refugees to that city, evidently enjoining a ship's captain to wait for them in England. He wrote that his ship was ready and waiting, for he did not want a single Religious of the Sacred Heart to be prevented from leaving.

8

PARIS AND AMERICA

ASSISTANT GENERAL

There never had been an American assistant general at the motherhouse, but in 1872, Mother Gœtz appointed Mother Hardey. She asked her to visit all the houses of the Society in North America: Canada, Cuba, and the United States, and to report in Paris by the end of the summer.[72]

Certain that knowledge of her appointment with its attendant separation would cause pain to all, she preferred to travel as visitator. At the age of sixty-two, she was setting out on a journey with an almost impossible timetable. Often plans had to be changed suddenly to suit available transportation, and there could be little warning in the days before the telephone. But when necessary, Mother Hardey did not mind arriving unannounced. In many respects her journey became a triumphant progress. She herself had founded most of the convents she now visited. She herself had trained many of the religious. From Eden Hall to Cincinnati,

---

72 Mother Gœtz wanted the convents of Europe and America to be united by a living link. To achieve this, she decided to appoint an American as assistant general, saying: "For such a *coup d'etat* I shall consult the Sovereign Pontiff, my Council, the clergy, the Jesuit missionaries, even the Father General." Williams, *Second Sowing*, p. 419.

from Detroit to St. Michael, from Havana to Halifax, the accounts of her visit breathe sincerest gratitude and affection. In Grand Coteau, the little room that had been the chapel when she took the habit in 1825 was arranged as it had been then.[73]

Because of the travel schedule, she was only able to stay at St. Michael for one day. She saw with pleasure the fine building there that had been still unfinished when she had left it thirty years before. "Old John," a former enslaved man of St. Michael, waited by the river for three nights to be sure to be there to welcome Mother Hardey, refusing to be replaced during his vigil. Mother Hardey had been at St. Michael when Mother Bazire had acquired a woman named Henny with her three small children: Mary, Joseph and John.[74] Another who eagerly awaited the return of Mother Hardey to St. Michael and was devastated at its brevity was Eliza Nebbit, longtime resident at St. Michael, first as enslaved, then as dedicated member of the household, now in her mid-sixties. She declared that Mother Hardey could not leave until she, Eliza, had the chance to open her soul to her.

There were 731 sisters and 146 novices in North America in 1872, and Mother Hardey probably saw them all. Her memory was phenomenal, so she probably remembered them all. It was said at the motherhouse that she knew the catalog by heart.

On the eve of her departure for Europe, she was still concerned with new foundations, and found time to visit a house in Providence, Rhode Island, soon to become Elmhurst. She noticed the

---

[73] At Grand Coteau, she recommended the opening of "a parochial or free school" for children of families ruined by the war (Superior's Memorial, Grand Coteau).

[74] Garvey, p. 313.

needs of the different houses and tried to satisfy them.[75] Finally, on September 11, 1872, she embarked for France, accompanied by her faithful secretary of many years, Mother Margaret Hoey. With her went two prospective novices, one of them her own half-sister Lena.[76] The separation from America was not to be as final as many feared, for three times during the next fourteen years, matters of business or health required her presence in New York. By this time, the crossing from New York could be done in as little as ten days. Mother Barat's "first American daughter" remained very much a part of her native land.

In Paris, after a brief respite from travel, as representative of Mother Gœtz, Mother Hardey visited the French convents of Bordeaux, Orléans and Beauvais, and went with her as companion to the foundation of Pau.[77] When Mother Gœtz died in 1874, she deeply felt the loss of this friend of many years.

VISIT TO AMERICA

Mother Adèle Lehon was elected superior general in May 1874. One of her first acts in office was to send Mother Hardey to New York to attend to urgent business regarding the Manhattanville property. A Supreme Court decision on taxes was due in October. "A question—was the land necessary for our works,"

---

75 Even as she was lavish with her gifts, Mother Hardey had a sharp eye for business. On a bill of Jan. 10, 1873, H. Erben, organ manufacturer, adds this postscript: "On account of Me. Hardey having ordered 4 organs from me I took $500 off my regular price."

76 When in May 1876, Mother Hardey learned of the death of this half-sister Lena, a novice at Manhattanville, her grief was such that only after an hour of prayer could she accept the loss.

77 The first photograph of a mother general was taken at Pau where Mother Hardey persuaded Mother Gœtz to pose with her. On this trip they visited the shrine of Our Lady of Lourdes. Williams, *Second Sowing*, p. 441.

Mother Hardey wrote, and later, "A definitive decision is due in January."[78] She remained nine months in America, finding time to visit many houses of her former vicariate. At Manhattanville, a reception was held for Archbishop McCloskey, newly created Cardinal, and with Mother Hardey present, he turned his speech into a eulogy of his friend of thirty years, while the priests attending expressed their own esteem and gratitude by a long ovation.

When Mother Hardey sailed again for France on April 20, 1875, she left without her secretary Mother Hoey, who literally had been her right hand for fourteen years. It was not Mother Hardey's wish, but that of Mother Lehon, for unknown reasons. This is clear from Mother Hardey's letter to Mother Lehon of February 19, 1875, responding to a letter from Mother Lehon written January 19 and no longer extant. How deeply Mother Hardey felt the sacrifice of Mother Hoey is evidenced in her letter: "I will not hide from you the fact that the sacrifice of my secretary costs very much...The change will cause extreme difficulty. No one can understand this, unless like me, they are dependent on another to express even what is most intimate." Then characteristically she concludes: "Since you desire it, I shall submit, and I shall try to find someone to replace."

We do not know why Mother Lehon wished Margaret Hoey to remain behind. She was perhaps too needed at home. Age thirty-six at the time, she had previously been involved with construction projects, and now immediately became vicariate treasurer.[79]

---

78 Sept. 29, 1874; Dec. 30, 1875. There would be more details of this interesting case, if fire had not destroyed most of the Manhattanville records in 1888, two years after Mother Hardey's death.

79 She later filled positions as assistant and superior at Madison Avenue and Elmhurst. She died at Arch Street, Philadelphia, in 1917.

To succeed Mother Hoey and return with Mother Hardey to Paris, she chose Pauline Seymour, who filled that service until 1882. In that capacity, she accompanied Mother Hardey in her travels in Spain and took copious and entertaining notes that filled in the missing spaces of the journey narrative.[80] It is not clear in the next two years who fulfilled that important position, but from 1884 to August 1886, it was Catherine Grasser, who was thus present for Mother Hardey's death in June, but remained at the motherhouse for two more months. She then returned to New York to take part in the foundation of Grosse Pointe, Michigan.[81]

---

80 Pauline Catherine Apolonie Seymour was born in Georgetown, Maryland, in 1843. Received into the Society by Mother Hardey, she entered at Kenwood, made her first vows there in 1869, and final profession there in December 1874. The following year she took up her position with Mother Hardey. After returning to New York in 1882, she devoted many years to instruction, especially to catechism classes in the free school. She died at Eden Hall in 1916.

81 Catherine Grasser, RSCJ, born 1843 in Dielkirk, Luxembourg, came to the United States as a child and entered the Society in 1859 at Manhattanville. She was finally professed in 1868 and served in several houses as assistant and treasurer, both before and after her secretarial position with Mother Hardey. She died in Rochester in 1918.

9

GOLDEN CONCLUSION

GOLDEN JUBILEE

In Paris once again, Mother Hardey continued her visits to the convents of France and Spain.[82] She began a new work in Beauvais, the Apostolic School, for the education of girls who desired religious life, but who needed financial help. Fundraising for this school occupied a large part of her time on subsequent visits to America. Even the celebration of her golden jubilee of first vows on March 15, 1877, was an occasion for receiving donations for this project.[83] Twelve trunkloads of gifts accompanied the American religious on their way to Paris that winter. From both sides of the Atlantic, friends of all ages sent congratulations, from her contemporary Cardinal McCloskey to the children of Manhattanville and Kenwood. Her co-worker in America for many years, Mother Amélie Jouve, came from Orléans for the celebration. The American novices at Conflans spent the day at

---

82 On the Spanish border she was treated with special courtesy, having been taken for the King's grandmother, Queen Cristina, traveling incognito.

83 The Golden Jubilee was usually the fiftieth anniversary of religious profession. Mother Hardey's decision to celebrate an earlier anniversary may have been prompted by the wish to avoid interference with Mother Lehon's Golden Jubilee of profession, which would have occurred the same summer as hers.

the motherhouse. Mother Hardey was visibly moved by these expressions of love and gratitude. "I wanted to weep," she said later, "if you had given me the time!" The schools in America received a holiday in her honor. There were Masses and panegyrics. At Manhattanville, Father F. J. L. Spalding, praising her gift for government, said, "She was born to rule, but to rule by the power of love and gentleness."[84] On this anniversary America was still very close to Mother Hardey.

OTHER VISITS

In 1878, a shorter visit to America restored her health, which was causing anxiety, and on her return to Conflans, Mother Hardey was given charge of the September group of probanists (young sisters preparing for final profession of vows) in Mother Juliette Desoudin's absence. This was a new responsibility for her, and she accepted it as she had every other throughout her life. She continued the visits to the convents of France and Belgium with Mother Lehon and acted as her interpreter in England and Ireland. In 1880, she was entrusted with the administration of the day school next to the motherhouse. Soon she was initiating a program for adult students, mostly American, "parlor boarders," as they were called.

In 1882 Mother Hardey made her last visit to America, in an attempt to save the Manhattanville property from the incursions of a rapidly growing city. Streets were being planned to cut through the grounds. Many felt that the convent should be moved. But Mother Hardey was determined to maintain both the location and the name of the school, which for forty years

---

84 Garvey, p. 341.

she had labored to make synonymous with fine education. It was a difficult assignment. She prayed long at Mother Barat's grave before setting out. She was now seventy-three years old. She had been away for ten years and was out of touch.

The negotiations lasted a year and a half, during which time she succeeded in selling some of the property and diverting the proposed street from the middle to the edge of the property. Friends who had formerly assisted her had moved away or died. But new friends came to her aid, and the buildings and grounds of the convent remained untouched by the city planners. For the last time, she had saved her beloved Manhattanville.

LAST FOUNDATIONS

Mother Hardey had seen the need for a day school in the central part of New York City, and in 1881, Cardinal McCloskey welcomed the Religious of the Sacred Heart to his cathedral parish and said the first Mass for them at Madison Avenue. The following year, Bishop Caspar Borgess of Detroit persuaded Mother Hardey to approve a second convent in his diocese at Grosse Pointe, the beautiful property on Lake St. Clair, which the Society had purchased in 1864.[85] In Atlantic City, Mother Hardey's long cherished hope for a convent by the sea for the health of the religious was fulfilled. The house had "everything we need" for an academy, she wrote to Mother Lehon on September 2, 1883. Soon she was planning for a parish school building, attending to every detail herself. Cardinal McCloskey visited the convent several times, his health noticeably improving

---

85 Garvey, p. 340. Mother Hardey did not live to see the completion of the academy building at Grosse Pointe, but she remained keenly interested in it. One of her concerns during her last illness was to make plans for the parish school to be erected there.

during the three weeks he spent there in 1883 with Mother Hardey. Mother Fanny Sullivan, writing to Mother Hardey later, on September 22, 1885, the year before her death, called the Atlantic City house "your favorite home," and "the last proof of your tender care."[86]

LEGACY

In February 1884, Mother Hardey sailed for France for the last time. The words welcoming her to New York on her arrival had expressed well the affectionate veneration in which she was held, "Your presence, your counsels, your encouragement, your love, your every word is enshrined in our hearts as a precious legacy." She had spent her life spreading the Society of the Sacred Heart in America and fostering its spirit of love. Her parting wish, summing up the inspiration of her own life, was that each one would, "live for, in, by, with the Sacred Heart."

DEATH

In Paris, Mother Hardey resumed her accustomed work until June 1885, when partial recuperation from an illness prompted a visit to the convent at Calais for sea air. On the way, she suffered a heart attack that left her only a few months of life. Now she traveled only in a wheelchair, for the first time inactive, until on June 19, 1886, God called her home. Mother Hardey was buried at Conflans near Mother Barat, but when the religious left France in 1905 during the political closing of Catholic

---

86 Frances Clotilde Sullivan, RSCJ (1852-1891), was in the Atlantic City house, according to the community register, from November 20, 1884, to January 20, 1886.

Reburial at Kenwood, 1905

institutions, her body was brought to America to rest in the cemetery at Kenwood.

Mother Barat from heaven must have looked at her with a loving smile and shared in the welcoming of her "first American daughter."

Ce Jourd'huy Vingt-neuf Avril, l'an de grace mil
Huit cent trente sept; et de l'indépendance des états-unis le
Soixante et unième.

　　　Entre les soussignés habitants de l'état de Louisiane
Paroisse St Jacques, Comté de l'Acadie; a été convenu, arrêté
et conclu ce qui suit.
　　　　　　　Savoir que

Dame Hardey (Alloysia) religieuse du Sacré Cœur,
et Supérieure de la maison de St Michel, agissant tant en
Son nom, et droits qui lui sont conférés, qu'au nom de
Dame Barat, Supérieure générale des dames du Sacré Cœur,
laquelle dame, et Vénérable Supérieure réside à Paris,
Royaume de France:　　　D'une part.

　　　& Prosper Amable Claudot Dumond, gérant de
la ferme modèle de l'état de la Louisiane, tant en son nom que
Comme caution, et se portant fort, pour le nommé Célestin
mulatre libre; présent acceptant et consentant.

　　　　　　Il a été dit

Que Dame Alloysia Hardey, Voulait bien prendre
en bonne part la Sollicitation qui lui était adressée par le
nommé Célestin pour l'affranchissement de Sa tante Françoise

　　　Que Dame Alloysia Hardey, en égard à l'âge
avancé, et aux Services de l'esclave Françoise, Comme aussi pour
répondre aux louables intentions de Célestin, Consentait à ce que
ladite esclave devint libre et affranchie.

　　　Toutefois, attendu que Dame Alloysia Hardey
Suffisamment autorisée à faire des concessions, ne se croit pas
munie de pouvoirs assez généraux pour faire des dons gratuits
Sans autorisation Spéciale, et que le retour de cette autorisation
d'ailleurs, mènerait à de trop longs délais au préjudice du
Sollicitant; Il a été convenu, qu'on pas à titre de

rachat, ou de payement, mais à titre d'indemnité, il sera
compté la somme de Cent piastres, au couvent des St. Michel,
par Célestin, le jour de la sortie et affranchissement de sa
tante françoise.

— Il est expressement arrêté, et Dame Alloysia
Hardey, en fait une condition expresse et dirigeant, qu'en
bien que l'indemnité de Cent piastres doive être comptée par
Célestin, la négresse françoise est et demeure à toujours libre
et affranchie, sans que le dit Célestin puisse jamais exercer
contre elle à aucun titre, acte d'épouvoir, possession, ou
autorité; ni même de demande légale en remboursement, tant
par lui qu'par ses ayant cause.

Toutes les conditions ci dessus sous acceptée par Célestin,
et le Sieur Claudot Dumon se porte comme caution de
l'exactitude de leur accomplissement.

L'exécution des conventions recevra son plein effet
dès le payement des Cent piastres mentionné et stipulé
au présent acte; et le Contrat deviendra régulier par la
quittance que Dame Alloysia Hardey apposera au bas
des présentes.

Célestin déclare devant les témoins qu'il ne sait pas
écrire; et quel signe de la croix qu'il apposera à sa signature
habituelle. La Présente fait à trois exemplaires entre nous
Soussignés. Lesjours et an que dessus.

F. A. Claudot Dumon   +   Aloysia Hardey

Signatures des témoins.
Samuel Fagot   F. Boué

Je soussignée, Supérieure du Couvent de St. Michel, Certifie avoir
reçu de Célestin Cent piastres Conformément au Contrat ci dessus
dont quittance.   P.ll. St. Jacques le 2 may 1837
                              Aloysia Hardey

Enfranchisement document of Françoise, St. Michael, 29 April, 1837. Page 2

APPENDIX

DOCUMENT ENFRANCHISING FRANÇOISE
APRIL 29, 1837

This day the 29 April, the year of grace 1837, and of the independence of the United States the 61st.

Between the undersigned residents of the State of Louisiana, Parish of St. James, County of Acadia; it has been agreed, established, and decided as follows.

Know that
Dame Hardey (Alloysia) [sic] religious of the Sacred Heart and Superior of the house of St. Michael, acting in her own name and by the rights conferred on her, in the name of Dame Barat, Superior general of the Dames du Sacré Coeur, which Dame and Venerable Superior resides in Paris, Kingdom of France:

On one part
And Prosper Amable Claudot Dumont, bearer of the seal of the state of Louisiana, in his name and for security, in full

authority, for the said Celestin, free mulatto, present, accepting and consenting.

It is said
that Dame Alloysia Hardey wishes to favor the request addressed to her by the said Celestin regarding the enfranchisement of his aunt Françoise,
that Dame Alloysia Hardey, in consideration of the advanced age, and of the services of the enslaved Françoise, and also to reply to the praiseworthy intentions of Celestin, consents that the said enslaved person become free and enfranchised.

However, since Dame Alloysia Hardey, sufficiently authorized to make concessions, does not believe herself invested with powers sufficiently general to make free gifts without special authorization, and that to await the return of this valid authorization would lead to a too long delay to the disadvantage of the petitioner, it has been agreed that, not as redemption or payment but as indemnity, the sum of one hundred piastres [dollars] will be deposited at the Convent of St. Michael by Celestin on the day of the emancipation of his aunt Françoise.

It is expressly stated, and Dame Alloysia Hardey, in virtue of an express and directive condition, that because of the indemnity of one hundred piastres paid by Celestin, the negress Françoise is and remains forever free and emancipated, and that the said Celestin is excluded from ever exercising against her any claim, act of power, possession, or authority, not even a legal expectation of reimbursement, either by him or by anyone for him.

All of the above conditions are accepted by Celestin, and Mister Claudot Dumond will have oversight of the exactitude of their accomplishment.

The execution of the agreement will receive full effect with the payment of the one hundred piastres, enacted and stipulated by the present act, and the contract will become enacted by the quittance that Dame Alloysia Hardey will put with the record of those present.

Celestin declares before witnesses that he cannot write, and that the mark of the cross which he will make is his habitual signature.

The present made in three copies by the undersigned, the day and year as above.

P.A. Claudot Dumont + Aloysia Hardey

Signatures of the witnesses

Samuel Fagot   L. Boué

I the undersigned, Superior of the Convent of St. Michael, certify having received from Celestin a hundred piastres in conformity with the above contract of which I am quit.

P-sse St. Jacques – 2 May, 1837 Aloysia Hardey

(Translation: C. Osiek)

SELECT BIBILOGRAPHY

ARCHIVAL MATERIAL, LETTERS, CATALOGUES

International Archives of the Society of the Sacred Heart, Rome

Provincial Archives of the Society of the Sacred Heart, United States-Canada Province, St. Louis, Missouri

Catalogues of the Society of the Sacred Heart

Lettres annuelles de la Société du Sacré-Cœur (Annual Letters, accounts of communities)

BOOKS

Baunard, Louis. *Histoire de la Vénérable Mère Madeleine Sophie Barat.* 2 Vols. Paris: Ch. Poussielgue, 1900.

Cahier, Adèle, RSCJ. *Vie de la Vénérable Mère Barat.* 2 Vols. Paris: De Soye, 1884.

Callan, Louise, RSCJ. *The Society of the Sacred Heart in North America.* New York: Longmans, 1937.

Dufour, Marie, RSCJ. *Vie de la Très Révérende Mère Marie-Joséphine Gœtz.* Roehampton, 1895.

Dufour, Marie, RSCJ. *Vie de la Très Révérende Mère Adèle Lehon.* Roehampton, 1895.

Dufour, Marie, RSCJ. *Vie de la Révérende Mère Mary Ann Aloysia Hardey.* Paris: Maison Mère, 1887.

Garvey, Mary, RSCJ. *Mary Aloysia Hardey.* New York: America Press, 1910; 2nd Edition, 1925.

Williams, Margaret, RSCJ. *Saint Madeleine Sophie: Her Life and Letters.* New York: Herder and Herder, 1965.

Williams, Margaret, RSCJ. *Second Sowing: The Life of Mary Aloysia Hardey.* New York: Sheed and Ward, 1942.

Note: Another short biography of Aloysia Hardey, by Carolyn Osiek, RSCJ, in *Southward, Ho! The Society of the Sacred Heart Enters "Lands of the Spanish Sea."* Ed. Marie Louise Martinez, RSCJ, pp. 37-60.

ACKNOWLEDGEMENTS IN THE ORIGINAL 1981 EDITION

Grateful acknowledgement of assistance:

Research: Mary Cecilia Wheeler, R.S.C.J., former Archivist of the International Archives of the Society of the Sacred Heart, Rome, Italy.

Marie-Louise Martinez, R.S.C.J., Archivist of the National Archives of the Society of the Sacred Heart, U.S.A., St. Louis, Missouri, U.S.A.

Cover Design: Harriot Benoist, R.S.C.J.

Preparation of Manuscript: Mary Parkinson, R.S.C.J.

ACKNOWLEDGEMENTS
IN THE REVISED EDITION

Michael Pera and Mary Charlotte Chandler, RSCJ, Provincial Archives, Society of the Sacred Heart, St. Louis, Missouri, for answers to numbers of small questions.

Provincial Publications Committee, USC Province, for support and encouragement.

www.ingramcontent.com/pod-product-compliance
Lightning Source LLC
LaVergne TN
LVHW051219070526
838200LV00064B/4971

प्राकृतिक आपदाओं को समझना

एम.पी.ए.-01

Notes For
Post Graduate Diploma in Disaster Management (PGDDM)

Useful For

IGNOU, KSOU (Karnataka), Bihar University (Muzaffarpur), Nalanda University, Jamia Millia Islamia, Vardhman Mahaveer Open University (Kota), Uttarakhand Open University, Kurukshetra University, Seva Sadan's College of Education (Maharashtra), Lalit Narayan Mithila University, Andhra University, Pt. Sunderlal Sharma (Open) University (Bilaspur), Annamalai University, Bangalore University, Bharathiar Univer sity, Bharathidasan University, HP University, Centre for distance and open learning, Kakatiya University (Andhra Pradesh), KOU (Rajasthan), MPBOU (MP), MDU (Haryana), Punjab University, Tamilnadu Open University, Sri Padmavati Mahila Visvavidyalayam (Andhra Pradesh), Sri Venkateswara University (Andhra Pradesh), UCSDE (Kerala), University of Jammu, YCMOU, Rajasthan University, UPRTOU, Kalyani University, Banaras Hindu University (BHU) and all other Indian Universities.

GullyBaba Publishing House Pvt. Ltd.

ISO 9001 & ISO 14001 CERTIFIED CO.

Regd. Office:
2525/193, 1st Floor, Onkar Nagar-A,
Tri Nagar, Delhi-110035
(From Kanhaiya Nagar Metro Station Towards Old Bus Stand)
Call: 9991112299, 9312235086
WhatsApp: 9350849407

Branch Office:
1A/2A, 20, Hari Sadan,
Ansari Road, Daryaganj,
New Delhi-110002
Ph.011-45794768
Call & WhatsApp:
8130521616, 8130511234

E-mail: hello@gullybaba.com, **Website**: GullyBaba.com

New Edition

Author: Gullybaba.com Panel

Copyright© with Publisher
All rights are reserved. No part of this publication may be reproduced or stored in a retrieval system or transmitted in any form or by any means; electronic, mechanical, photocopying, recording or otherwise, without the written permission of the copyright holder.

Disclaimer
Although the author and publisher have made every effort to ensure that the information in this notes is correct, the author and publisher do not assume and hereby disclaim any liability to any party for any loss, damage, or disruption caused by errors or omissions, whether such errors or omissions result from negligence, accident, or any other cause.

If you find any kind of error, please let us know and get reward and or the new notes free of cost.

The notes is based on IGNOU syllabus. This is only a sample. The notes/author/publisher does not impose any guarantee or claim for full marks or to be passed in exam. You are advised only to understand the contents with the help of this notes and answer in your words.

All disputes with respect to this publication shall be subject to the jurisdiction of the Courts, Tribunals and Forums of New Delhi, India only.